Albatross to Zebra Finch

Birds from A to Z

Mary Elizabeth Salzmann

Consulting Editor, Diane Craig, M.A./Reading Specialist

ABDO
Publishing Company

Published by ABDO Publishing Company, 8000 West 78th Street, Edina, Minnesota 55439. Copyright © 2009 by Abdo Consulting Group, Inc. International copyrights reserved in all countries. No part of this book may be reproduced in any form without written permission from the publisher. Super SandCastle™ is a trademark and logo of ABDO Publishing Company.

Printed in the United States.

Editor: Pam Price
Content Developer: Nancy Tuminelly
Cover and Interior Design and Production: Colleen Dolphin, Mighty Media
Photo Credits: Mike Danzenbaker, Karen Hughes, BIOS Dennis Nigel J./Peter Arnold, Shutterstock

Library of Congress Cataloging-in-Publication Data

Salzmann, Mary Elizabeth, 1968-
  Albatross to zebra finch : birds from A to Z / Mary Elizabeth Salzmann.
    p. cm. -- (Let's look A to Z)
  ISBN 978-1-60453-009-4
  1. Birds--Juvenile literature. 2. English language--Alphabet--Juvenile literature. I. Title.

QL676.2.S24 2009
590--dc22

                      2007050940

Super SandCastle™ books are created by a team of professional educators, reading specialists, and content developers around five essential components— phonemic awareness, phonics, vocabulary, text comprehension, and fluency— to assist young readers as they develop reading skills and strategies and increase their general knowledge. All books are written, reviewed, and leveled for guided reading, early reading intervention, and Accelerated Reader® programs for use in shared, guided, and independent reading and writing activities to support a balanced approach to literacy instruction.

About Super SandCastle™

Bigger Books for Emerging Readers Grades K-4

Created for library, classroom, and at-home use, Super SandCastle™ books support and engage young readers as they develop and build literacy skills and will increase their general knowledge about the world around them. Super SandCastle™ books are part of SandCastle™, the leading preK–3 imprint for emerging and beginning readers. Super SandCastle™ features a larger trim size for more reading fun.

Let Us Know

Super SandCastle™ would like to hear your stories about reading this book. What was your favorite page? Was there something hard that you needed help with? Share the ups and downs of learning to read. We want to hear from you! Send us an e-mail.

sandcastle@abdopublishing.com

Contact us for a complete list of SandCastle™, Super SandCastle™, and other nonfiction and fiction titles from ABDO Publishing Company.

www.abdopublishing.com • 8000 West 78th Street Edina, MN 55439 • 800-800-1312 • 952-831-1632 fax

This fun and informative series employs illustrated definitions to introduce emerging readers to an alphabet of words in various topic areas. Each page combines words with corresponding images and descriptive sentences to encourage learning and knowledge retention. AlphagalorZ inspires young readers to find out more about the subjects that most interest them!

The "Guess what?" feature expands the reading and learning experience by offering additional information and fascinating facts about specific words or concepts. The "More Words" section provides additional related A to Z vocabulary words that develop and increase reading comprehension.

These books are appropriate for library, classroom, and home use.

Aa

Guess what?

The wandering albatross has a larger wingspan than any other bird.

Albatross

Albatross are large seabirds. There are many different species of albatross.

They live near the Southern Ocean and the North Pacific Ocean.

black-browed albatross

Bluebird

Bluebirds are found in North America and South America.

They live in areas with open grassland and few trees.

mountain bluebird

Guess what?

The mountain bluebird is the state bird of Idaho and Nevada.

Bb

5

Cockatoo

Cockatoos are related to parrots.

The group of long feathers on a cockatoo's head is called a crest.

cockatiel

Guess what?

The cockatiel is a species of cockatoo that is often kept as a pet.

Cc

Duck

Ducks can be found anywhere in the world that has water.

Diving ducks can swim deep underwater to find food.

Dabbling ducks eat food found near the top of the water or on land.

mallard

Eagle

Eagles are large birds that hunt small animals such as mice and rabbits.

They have large hooked beaks and strong talons.

Eagles use their excellent eyesight to find prey.

Ee

bald eagle

Caribbean flamingo

Flamingo

Flamingos are tall wading birds that live in warm climates.

They dip their special beaks into the water upside down to scoop food from the ocean floor.

Flamingos get their pink color from the shrimp they eat.

Ff

Guess what?

Flamingos often stand on one leg, and no one knows why.

9

herring gull

Gg

Gull

Gulls are seabirds that live near coasts, rivers, and lakes.

They are usually gray or white with black markings.

Gulls will drop clams from high in the air to break open the shells.

Guess what?

Gulls sometimes steal food from each other.

10

Hummingbird

Hummingbirds can hover in the air and can even fly backward.

They have long beaks that they stick into flowers to feed on the nectar.

Guess what?

The bee hummingbird is the smallest bird in the world.

Anna's hummingbird

11

Ibis

Ibis are wading birds that live in warm climates.

They use their large curved beaks to dig in mud and shallow water to find food.

glossy ibis

li

12

java sparrow

Jj

Java Sparrow

Java sparrows are native to Asia but have spread to other parts of the world.

They are also called rice birds because rice is one of their favorite foods.

Kk

laughing kookaburra

Kookaburra

Kookaburras live in Australia and New Guinea.

They are named kookaburra after their call, which can sound like human laughter.

Guess what?

A kookaburra was one of the mascots of the 2000 Summer Olympics in Sydney, Australia.

Loon

Guess what?

The common loon is the state bird of Minnesota.

Loons can dive more than 200 feet underwater to catch fish to eat.

Baby loons often ride on the back of their mothers or fathers.

common loon

15

Macaw

Macaws are members of the parrot family that live in Mexico, Central America, and South America.

They nest inside hollow trees or holes in cliffs.

Mm

Guess what?

The hyacinth macaw has a wingspan greater than four feet.

blue-and-yellow macaw

Nuthatch

Nuthatches live in forests in the Northern Hemisphere.

They wedge nuts in tree notches and peck at them to crack the shells.

Guess what?

Unlike most birds, nuthatches can walk headfirst down tree trunks.

white-breasted nuthatch

Nn

yellow-eyed owl

Owl

Owls can see very well in the dark and hunt for food at night.

They also have excellent hearing and sometimes find prey by sound.

Guess what?

Owls sometimes swallow their prey whole.

Penguin

Penguins cannot fly. Instead, they use their wings like flippers to help them swim.

Penguins recognize their mates and chicks by their calls.

Guess what?

Penguins spend over half their lives in the sea.

Adelie penguin

Qq

Quail

Quail spend most of their time on the ground, hidden in long grass.

They will fly when startled but usually run away from danger.

Guess what..?

A group of quail is called a covey.

California quail

20

Roadrunner

Roadrunners live in deserts in North America and Central America.

They can run as fast as 18 miles per hour.

Guess what?

The roadrunner is the state bird of New Mexico.

greater roadrunner

21

Swan

Swans are the largest waterfowl.

They can be white, black, or black-and-white.

A male swan is called a cob, a female swan is a pen, and a baby swan is a cygnet.

mute swan

Ss

Guess what?

Swans can live longer than 20 years.

keel-billed toucan

Toucan

Toucans live in Mexico, Central America, and South America.

They are known for their large, brightly colored beaks.

Toucans nest inside holes in trees.

Tt

23

Uu

Upland Sandpiper

Upland sandpipers live on grasslands and prairies.

They like to perch on stumps, fence posts, and telephone poles.

upland sandpiper

lappet-faced vulture

Vulture

Vultures are scavengers. They eat animals that are already dead rather than hunt for prey.

They soar high in the air for hours at a time looking for food.

Guess what?

Most vultures have bald heads.

Vv

pileated woodpecker

Guess what?

Tapping is also a way woodpeckers communicate with each other.

Woodpecker

Woodpeckers tap holes in trees with their beaks to find food.

They have very long, barbed tongues that they stick into the holes to grab insects.

W w

Xantus's Murrelet

Xantus's murrelets breed on islands in the Pacific Ocean near California and Mexico.

They dive underwater to catch fish to eat.

Guess what?

Xantus's murrelet chicks leave their nests and run into the ocean when they are just two days old.

Xantus's murrelet

Yellow Canary

The yellow canary is
a species of finch that
lives in southern Africa.

Yellow canaries build
their nests in low trees
and bushes.

Guess what?

A yellow canary's
nest is shaped like
a little cup.

yellow canary

28

Zebra Finch

Zebra finches come from Australia and Indonesia.

Male zebra finches sing loudly, and each bird's song is unique.

Female zebra finches can't sing.

zebra finch

Glossary

barbed – having one or more sharp points that stick out and backward.

breed – to create offspring or babies.

climate – the usual weather in a place.

communicate – to share ideas, information, or feelings.

crest – the upright, decorative feathers on top of a bird's head.

female – being of the sex that can produce eggs or give birth. Mothers are female.

finch – one of many kinds of songbirds that eat seeds and grains.

flipper – a wide, flat limb of a sea creature, such as a seal or a dolphin, that is used for swimming.

grassland – a large area of land covered with grasses.

hemisphere – one half of the earth.

insect – a small creature with two or four wings, six legs, and a body with three sections.

laughter – a sound you make that lets others know you are happy or amused.

male – being of the sex that can father offspring. Fathers are male.

marking – the usual pattern of color on an animal.

mascot – a person, animal, or object that is supposed to bring good luck to a team or an organization.

notch – a V-shaped cut or gap.

prey – an animal that is hunted or caught for food.

scavenger – one that feeds on whatever garbage or dead animals it finds.

shrimp – a small shellfish often caught for food.

soar – to fly high in the sky.

species – a group of related living beings.

symbol – an object that represents something else.

talon – the claw of an animal, especially that of a bird of prey.

unique – the only one of its kind.

unlike – different or not alike.

wingspan – the distance from one wing tip to the other when the wings are fully spread.

More Birds!

Can you learn about these birds too?

avocet	goose	pelican
bittern	grouse	pheasant
blackbird	hawk	pigeon
blue jay	heron	puffin
bunting	jacana	quetzal
buzzard	kestrel	razorbill
cardinal	kingfisher	robin
condor	lark	sparrow
cormorant	linnet	starling
crane	magpie	stork
crow	mockingbird	swallow
cuckoo	nightingale	swift
dove	oriole	tern
egret	osprey	thrush
emu	ostrich	turkey
falcon	parakeet	warbler
finch	parrot	wren
gannet	partridge	yellowhammer